MATHS ACTIVITIES
FOR THE NATIONAL CURRICULUM

Compiled and edited by
Thelma Aspin
Christine Brown
Ray Fraser
Gerry Price
Ian Roper

Copymasters 1
— *covering Level 4 of the National Curriculum*

EPL

EGON PUBLISHERS LTD
Royston Road, Baldock, Hertfordshire SG7 6NW, England

First published in the United Kingdom
in November 1989
by Egon Publishers Ltd
Royston Road, Baldock, Hertfordshire SG7 6NW, England

Copyright © Egon Publishers Ltd
and the authors
Thelma Aspin, Christine Brown, Ray Fraser,
Gerry Price and Ian Roper

ISBN 0 905858 52 2

Designed, typeset and printed for the publishers
by Streetsprinters, Royston Road, Baldock, Hertfordshire SG7 6NW England

INTRODUCTION

This set of Copymasters is produced as a companion to *Maths Activities for the National Curriculum, Book 1*. This book outlines activities related to each of the Statements of Attainment at Level 4 and certain of these require worksheets for use by pupils. Each Copymaster is coded in the top right hand corner with the number of the activity for which it is intended.

Additionally, Copymasters are provided for the production of grid papers which are commonly used in mathematics classrooms. All Copymasters may be freely copied for use by pupils in the educational establishment which purchased them.

PHOTOCOPYING OF THIS WORK

All rights reserved. The publisher hereby grants photocopying rights of this work for use with the 'Maths Activities for the National Curriculum' Teachers' Resource Book 1. Otherwise, no part of this book may be reproduced or transmitted in any form or by any means, electronic or mechanical, including recording or by any information storage or retrieval system without permission in writing from the publisher.

CALENDAR

	JANUARY					
S	M	Tu	W	Th	F	S

	FEBRUARY					
S	M	Tu	W	Th	F	S

	MARCH					
S	M	Tu	W	Th	F	S

	APRIL					
S	M	Tu	W	Th	F	S

	MAY					
S	M	Tu	W	Th	F	S

	JUNE					
S	M	Tu	W	Th	F	S

	JULY					
S	M	Tu	W	Th	F	S

	AUGUST					
S	M	Tu	W	Th	F	S

	SEPTEMBER					
S	M	Tu	W	Th	F	S

	OCTOBER					
S	M	Tu	W	Th	F	S

	NOVEMBER					
S	M	Tu	W	Th	F	S

	DECEMBER					
S	M	Tu	W	Th	F	S

LESS THAN

You will need: to cut out the individual cards

17 000	<	16 080	<	16 800	<	16 008	<
18 060	<	18 007	<	89 701	<	89 071	<
123 580	<	135 008	<	908 002	<	980 002	<
7 605	<	7 650	<	7 065	<	380 000	<
38 000	<	30 008	<	57 050	<	50 750	<
900 000	<	9 000	<	100 010	<	190 010	<
590 040	<	950 004	<	590 004	<	78 625	<
893 470	<	68 580	<	375 624	<	872 638	<
5 847	<	6 893	<	2 715	<	31 257	<
1 MILLION		1 MILLION		1 MILLION		1 MILLION	

2a

2b

DIAMOND SEARCH — an investigation for one player

You will need: a calculator

A company are mining a diamond field. They mine each square section of the field in turn. They always move from one square to the next across a line, never diagonally. This grid shows the profit in pounds they can earn from mining each square.

108 849	619 681	159 701	150 051	17 000
113 660	77 121	15 709	16 185 → 100 512	
20 000	6 059	START	→ 30 987	288 900
9 823	7 981	10 099	9 004	56 200
358 007	93 500	300 067	409 090	9 070

The trail marked on the grid would give a profit of £164 684

£30 987 + £16 185 + £100 512 + £17 000

Investigate which route the mining company should take to make the highest profit after mining four squares.

LOLLY STICKS — a game for two players

You will need: 14 lolly sticks

In this game your numbers must look like the numbers on a calculator.

0123456789

Decide who goes first.

Use the lolly sticks to make the number 88.

88

The first player moves two lolly sticks to make a higher number, e.g. 138.

138

The second player also moves two lolly sticks to make an even higher number, e.g. 381.

381

From now on take turns to tell your opponent to make a higher or lower number.

Your opponent may choose to move either one or two sticks to do so.

Numbers made previously cannot be repeated.

The game continues until one of you cannot go. The other player is the winner.

HEXALINES — a multiplication game for two players

You will need: 25 black and 25 white counters
2 ordinary dice
a calculator

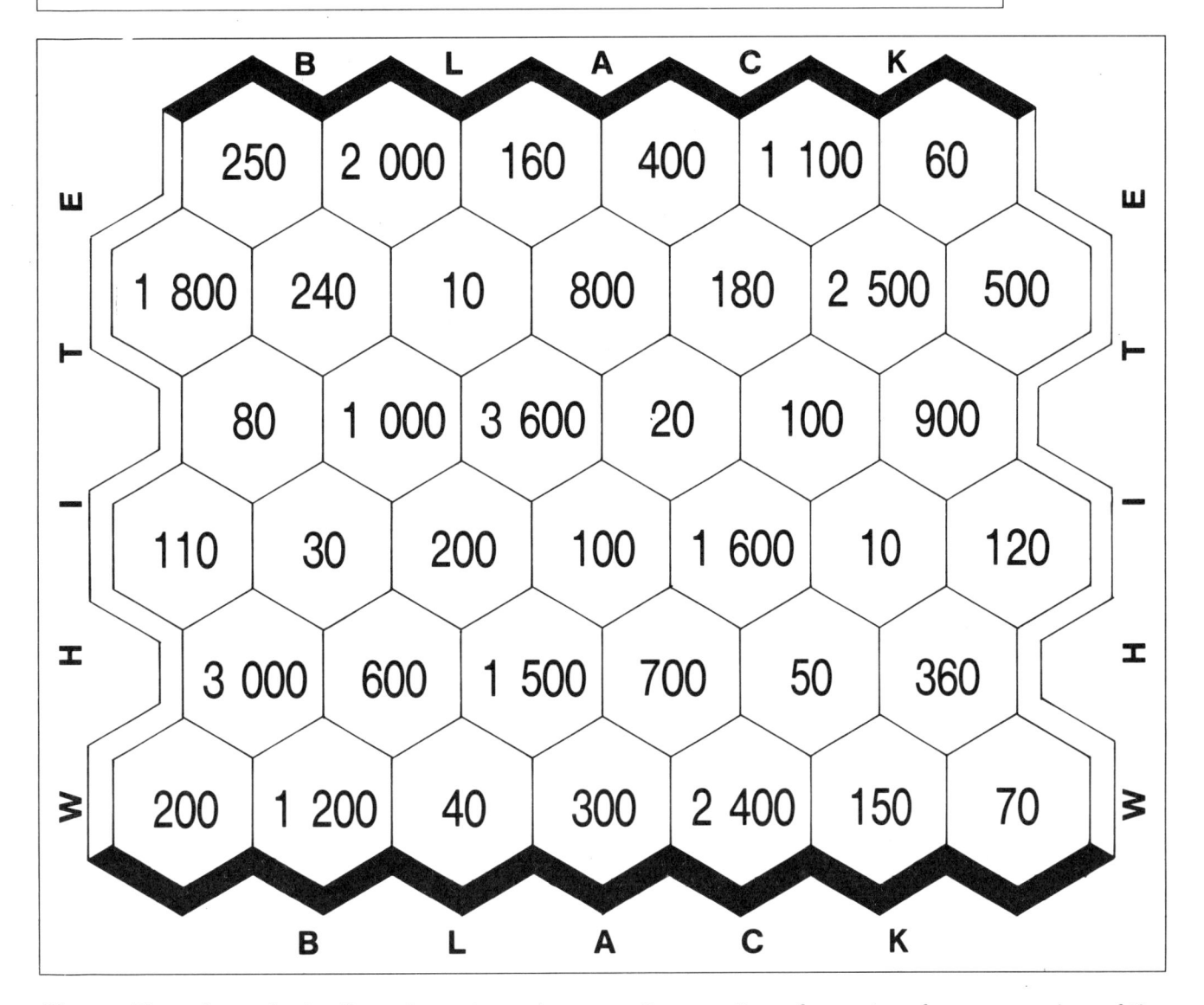

```
            B     L     A     C     K
         250  2 000  160   400  1 100   60
E                                                E
      1 800  240    10    800   180  2 500  500
T                                                T
         80  1 000 3 600   20   100   900
I                                                I
        110   30   200    100  1 600   10   120
H                                                H
      3 000  600  1 500   700   50   360
W                                                W
        200  1 200  40    300  2 400  150    70
            B     L     A     C     K
```

Aim — The winner is the first player to make a continuous line of counters from one edge of the board to the opposite edge.

How to play
1. Decide who will go first. The first player must try to get from left to right (WHITE to WHITE). The second player must try to get from top to bottom (BLACK to BLACK).
2. Take turns to throw both dice. You may add, subtract, multiply or divide the two dice scores to get your start number.
3. Look at the numbers on the board. Multiply your start number by 10 or 100 to try to make one of the numbers on the board. If you can make one of the numbers, explain to your opponent how you made it and place one of your counters on that hexagon.
4. If you cannot make one of the numbers the turn passes to your opponent.

FIND THE PAIRS — a number search for one

TIMES TEN — Search through the grid below putting a loop around those pairs of numbers where one number is TEN TIMES the other. There are twelve pairs. One is done for you.

29	36	−24	−32	49	26
10	290	115	96	−320	1
1	9	960	25	3	60
260	4	40	−2 000	250	5
2 600	−30	−200	−50	90	260
−3	69	690	−500	26	9

TIMES A HUNDRED — Search through the grid below putting a loop around those pairs of numbers where one number is ONE HUNDRED TIMES the other. There are twelve pairs.

42	16	−95	15	37	300
17	4 200	−9 500	3 700	3	28
1 000	1 700	−500	9	2 800	100
80	10	16	−5 000	1 200	1
6	8	800	160	−600	12
60	4 500	45	6	120	−6

DOMINOES

100	25×100	220×10	500	1000	180×10	70×10	3600
5000	36×100	1500	360×10	1800	35×100	45×100	100
27×100	2200	2500	15×100	500×10	2700	4500	100×10
150×10	3500	10×100	1800	270×10	10000	350×10	2500
10×10	10000	700	100×100	1000×10	5000	50×10	2200
22×100	1000	50×100	4500	1×100	3600	1500	7×100
500	450×10	250×10	2700	700	5×100	3500	18×100

OPERATION BINGO

3a/1

2×6	36÷9	9×9	4×8	3×6	7×9	4×6	5×8	6×7
5×7	2×7	7×8	9×6	70÷7	36÷6	18÷9	5×9	4×8
6×8	40÷8	3×9	2×8	5×9	3×7	7×7	24÷6	3×9
2×7	5×6	8×8	3×6	10×8	5×7	6×6	10×7	2×8
2×6	42÷7	3×9	3×7	72÷6	6×9	9×8	40÷8	5×9
10×8	5×9	60÷6	80÷8	4×8	9×9	2×6	4×7	72÷9
2×6	5×9	42÷7	2×9	8×7	6×9	16÷8	7×6	3×7
4×6	36÷6	4×8	8×8	24÷6	2×7	7×7	4×8	81÷9
9×9	6×7	2×8	4×6	63÷9	5×8	4×9	2×6	7×8
3×9	6×6	12÷6	5×9	7×9	3×6	54÷9	2×6	10×9
6×8	9×6	8×9	5×6	32÷8	10×8	4×8	5×6	18÷6
80÷8	10×6	2×8	2×9	7×8	35÷7	3×9	3×7	8×8

OPERATION BINGO

THREE IN A LINE — a multiplication game for two players

You will need: 2 dice
9 yellow counters
9 red counters

1	12	3	24	6	25
18	2	10	6	20	12
20	24	3	8	9	16
12	15	30	4	6	12
15	8	10	36	5	4
2	18	4	5	30	6

HOW TO PLAY

1. Decide who will go first and who will have which colour.
2. Take it in turns to throw the two dice.
3. The thrower works out the number obtained by multiplying the two numbers on the dice.
4. If the correct answer is given, then the thrower can cover up that number on the grid.
5. If an incorrect answer is given, then the other player can challenge and give the correct answer to claim the square.
6. Once a square has been covered up, it cannot be used again.
7. The first player to get three counters in a line is the winner.

PLAY THE GAME SEVERAL TIMES — WHO WON THE MOST GAMES?

FOLLOW ME

⑥	㉚	⑮	㉠60
ADD 24 FOLLOW ME	SUBTRACT 15 FOLLOW ME	MULTIPLY BY 4 FOLLOW ME	DIVIDE BY 3 FOLLOW ME
⑳	⑩⑩	㊆77	⑦
MULTIPLY BY 5 FOLLOW ME	SUBTRACT 23 FOLLOW ME	DIVIDE BY 11 FOLLOW ME	MULTIPLY BY 9 FOLLOW ME
63	84	12	108
ADD 21 FOLLOW ME	DIVIDE BY 7 FOLLOW ME	MULTIPLY BY 9 FOLLOW ME	SUBTRACT 59 FOLLOW ME
49	54	27	9
ADD 5 FOLLOW ME	DIVIDE BY 2 FOLLOW ME	DIVIDE BY 3 FOLLOW ME	ADD 36 FOLLOW ME
45	90	33	3
ADD 45 FOLLOW ME	SUBTRACT 57 FOLLOW ME	DIVIDE BY 11 FOLLOW ME	MULTIPLY BY 8 FOLLOW ME
24	65	35	5
ADD 41 FOLLOW ME	SUBTRACT 30 FOLLOW ME	DIVIDE BY 7 FOLLOW ME	MULTIPLY BY 2 FOLLOW ME
10	50	25	62
ADD 40 FOLLOW ME	DIVIDE BY 2 FOLLOW ME	ADD 37 FOLLOW ME	ADD 18 FOLLOW ME
80	8	72	36
DIVIDE BY 10 FOLLOW ME	MULTIPLY BY 9 FOLLOW ME	DIVIDE BY 2 FOLLOW ME	DIVIDE BY 6 FOLLOW ME

COVER UP — an estimation game for two players

You will need: 8 red counters
8 blue counters
a calculator

4 000	25 000	800	1 000
40 000	190	500	8 000
190	700	50 000	4 000
100	300	20 000	5 000

How to play:

1. Decide who will go first and who will have which colour.

2. Take it in turns to choose two of these numbers.

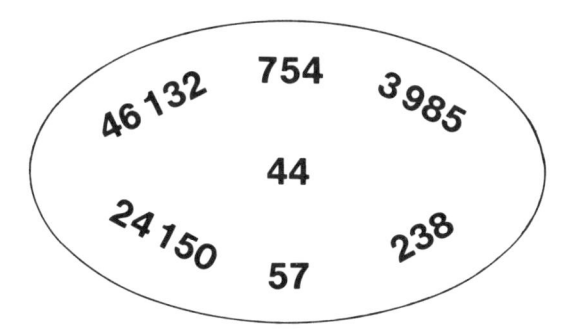

> 46 132   754   3 985
> 44
> 24 150   57   238

3. Decide whether to add or subtract your numbers.

4. Choose a number in one of the squares on the board which you think is a good rough (approximate) answer.

5. Check with a calculator. If the number you chose is a good approximation, cover the square with one of your counters.

6. The first to get a line of three counters is the winner.

PLAY THE GAME SEVERAL TIMES — WHO WON THE MOST GAMES?

EQUIVALENT FRACTIONS PUZZLE

Pick out all the letters which are joined to a fraction which equals one half.

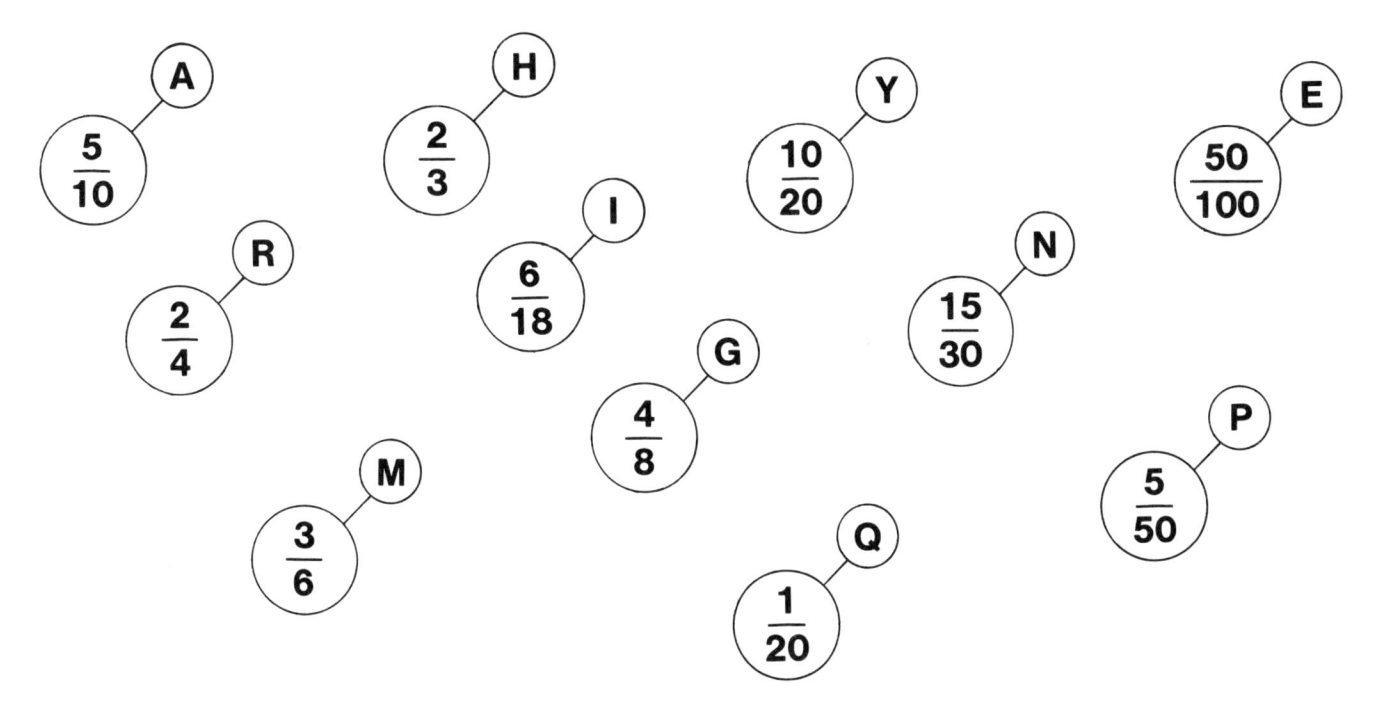

- $\frac{5}{10}$ — A
- $\frac{2}{3}$ — H
- $\frac{10}{20}$ — Y
- $\frac{50}{100}$ — E
- $\frac{2}{4}$ — R
- $\frac{6}{18}$ — I
- $\frac{15}{30}$ — N
- $\frac{4}{8}$ — G
- $\frac{3}{6}$ — M
- $\frac{1}{20}$ — Q
- $\frac{5}{50}$ — P

Re-arrange the letters you have picked out to make the name of a country.

_____

Pick out all the letters which are joined to a fraction which equals one third.

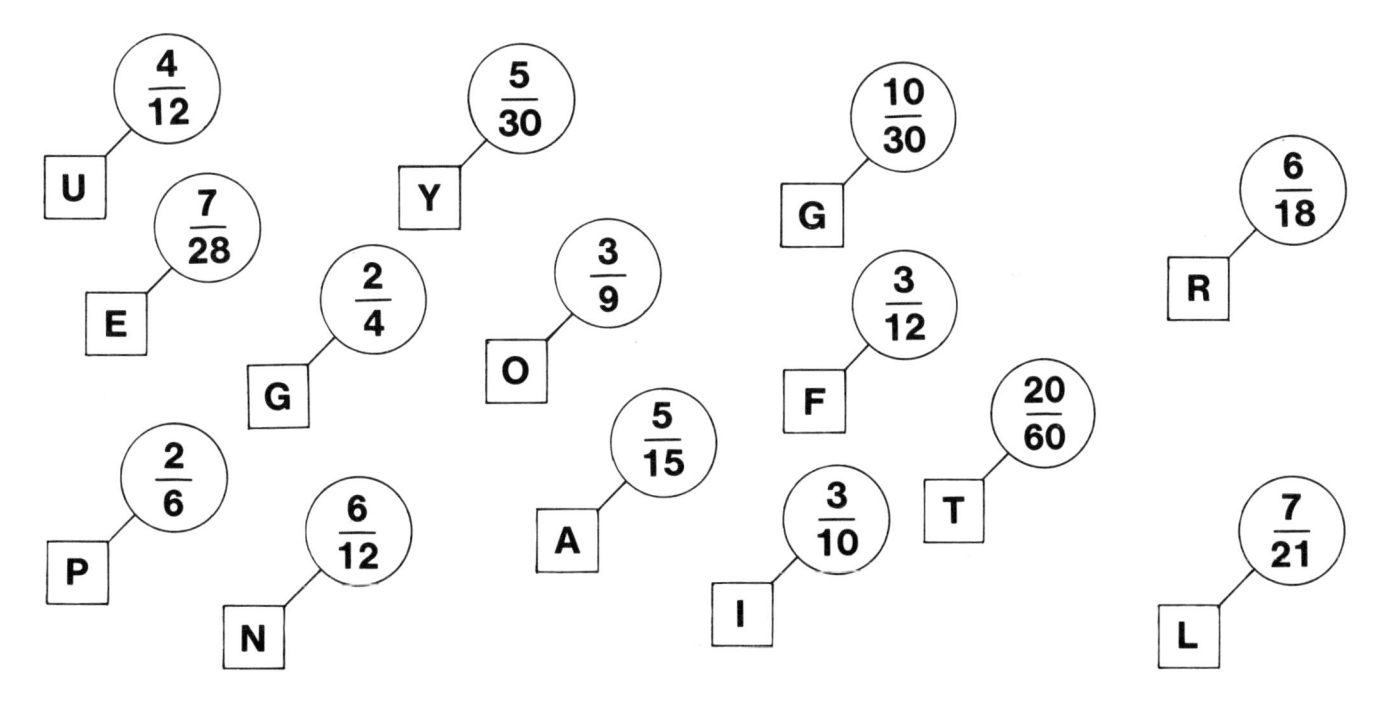

- $\frac{4}{12}$ — U
- $\frac{7}{28}$ — E
- $\frac{5}{30}$ — Y
- $\frac{2}{4}$ — G
- $\frac{3}{9}$ — O
- $\frac{10}{30}$ — G
- $\frac{3}{12}$ — F
- $\frac{6}{18}$ — R
- $\frac{2}{6}$ — P
- $\frac{6}{12}$ — N
- $\frac{5}{15}$ — A
- $\frac{3}{10}$ — I
- $\frac{20}{60}$ — T
- $\frac{7}{21}$ — L

Re-arrange the letters you have picked out to make the name of a country.

MULTIPLICATION SQUARE

1	2	3	4	5	6	7	8	9	10	11	12	13	14	15	16	17	18	19	20
2	4	6	8	10	12	14	16	18	20	22	24	26	28	30	32	34	36	38	40
3	6	9	12	15	18	21	24	27	30	33	36	39	42	45	48	51	54	57	60
4	8	12	16	20	24	28	32	36	40	44	48	52	56	60	64	68	72	76	80
5	10	15	20	25	30	35	40	45	50	55	60	65	70	75	80	85	90	95	100
6	12	18	24	30	36	42	48	54	60	66	72	78	84	90	96	102	108	114	120
7	14	21	28	35	42	49	56	63	70	77	84	91	98	105	112	119	126	133	140
8	16	24	32	40	48	56	64	72	80	88	96	104	112	120	128	136	144	152	160
9	18	27	36	45	54	63	72	81	90	99	108	117	126	135	144	153	162	171	180
10	20	30	40	50	60	70	80	90	100	110	120	130	140	150	160	170	180	190	200
11	22	33	44	55	66	77	88	99	110	121	132	143	154	165	176	187	198	209	220
12	24	36	48	60	72	84	96	108	120	132	144	156	168	180	192	204	216	228	240
13	26	39	52	65	78	91	104	117	130	143	156	169	182	195	208	221	234	247	260
14	28	42	56	70	84	98	112	126	140	154	168	182	196	210	224	238	252	266	280
15	30	45	60	75	90	105	120	135	150	165	180	195	210	225	240	255	270	285	300
16	32	48	64	80	96	112	128	144	160	176	192	208	224	240	256	272	288	304	320
17	34	51	68	85	102	119	136	153	170	187	204	221	238	255	272	289	306	323	340
18	36	54	72	90	108	126	144	162	180	198	216	234	252	270	288	306	324	342	360
19	38	57	76	95	114	133	152	171	190	209	228	247	266	285	304	323	342	361	380
20	40	60	80	100	120	140	160	180	200	220	240	260	280	300	320	340	360	380	400

RACE TRACK — a game for two or more players

You will need: A die
A red and a yellow counter

Board spaces (from START, around the track):

- START
- ADD 3
- TAKE 2
- MULTIPLY BY 2 AND TAKE 4
- ADD 2
- SUBTRACT 3
- DOUBLE AND ADD 1
- SUBTRACT FROM 6
- ADD 1 THEN MULTIPLY BY 2
- ADD 5
- SUBTRACT 3
- TAKE 3 THEN DOUBLE
- ADD 4
- MULTIPLY BY 3
- MULTIPLY BY 2 AND SUBTRACT FROM 12
- ADD 5
- SUBTRACT FROM 10
- ADD 2
- DOUBLE
- SUBTRACT FROM 8
- ADD 1 AND MULTIPLY BY 2
- MULTIPLY BY 4 AND SUBTRACT FROM 30
- ADD 2 AND SUBTRACT FROM 8
- ADD 3
- SUBTRACT 4
- FINISH

RULES

1. Decide who will go first and who will have which colour.
2. Take turns to throw the die.
3. Use your score and follow the instructions for the space your counter is on.
4. Move your counter forward the number of spaces resulting from your answer.
5. If you have a negative answer you will need to go backwards.
6. The winner is the first to complete 3 laps.

CO-ORDINATE BINGO

(4,8)	(4,9)	(5,0)	(5,1)
(5,2)	(5,3)	(5,4)	(5,5)
(5,6)	(5,7)	(5,8)	(5,9)
(6,0)	(6,1)	(6,2)	(6,3)
(6,4)	(6,5)	(6,6)	(6,7)
(6,8)	(6,9)	(7,0)	(7,1)
(7,2)	(7,3)	(7,4)	(7,5)
(7,6)	(7,7)	(7,8)	(7,9)
(8,0)	(8,1)	(8,2)	(8,3)
(8,4)	(8,5)	(8,6)	(8,7)
(8,8)	(8,9)	(9,0)	(9,1)
(9,2)	(9,3)	(9,4)	(9,5)
(9,6)	(9,7)	(9,8)	(9,9)

CO-ORDINATE BINGO

(0,0)	(0,1)	(0,2)	(0,3)
(0,4)	(0,5)	(0,6)	(0,7)
(0,8)	(0,9)	(1,0)	(1,1)
(1,2)	(1,3)	(1,4)	(1,5)
(1,6)	(1,7)	(1,8)	(1,9)
(2,0)	(2,1)	(2,2)	(2,3)
(2,4)	(2,5)	(2,6)	(2,7)
(2,8)	(2,9)	(3,0)	(3,1)
(3,2)	(3,3)	(3,4)	(3,5)
(3,6)	(3,7)	(3,8)	(3,9)
(4,0)	(4,1)	(4,2)	(4,3)
(4,4)	(4,5)	(4,6)	(4,7)

7a/2

TREASURE HUNT — a game for two players

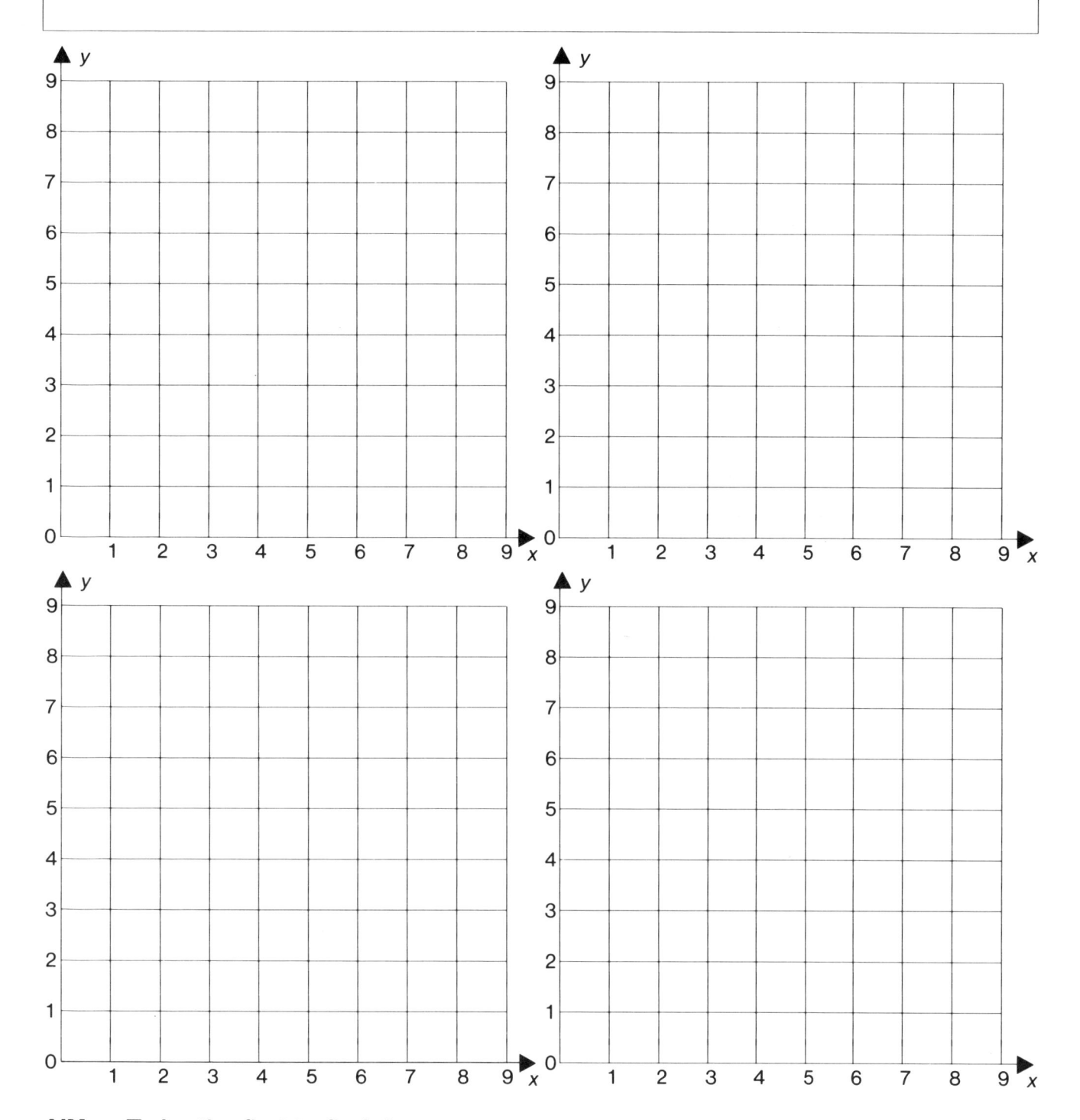

AIM — To be the first to find the treasure.

The grids show the streets of a city.

1. You will need to use TWO grids for each game.
2. On the left hand grid: Hide your treasure by marking a cross on any of the street corners. Do not let your opponent see.
3. Decide who will go first.
4. Take it in turns to say where you think your opponent has hidden the treasure, by giving the co-ordinates of a street corner. Use your right hand grid to record the guesses you make.
5. Mark your opponent's guesses with a small circle on your left hand grid. Tell your opponent how many blocks he or she is from the treasure.
6. The winner is the one who finds the opponent's treasure first.

8d

HOW LONG DOES IT TAKE?

Look at the six pictures. They show six activities that the boy has to do before he gets to school.

1. Decide what the correct order should be for the pictures.
2. Estimate how long it would take the boy to do each activity.

CAR SURVEY

You are to design and carry out a survey of cars and use your results to comment on these two statements:

"Most cars on the road today are foreign."
"The average age of a car is six years."

CAR SURVEY INFORMATION SHEET

British Cars		Foreign Cars	
Aston Martin	M.G.	Alfa-Romeo	Moskvich
Austin	Mini	Audi	Nissan
Austin-Healey	Morgan	BMW	N.S.U.
Bentley	Morris	Citroen	Opel
Chrysler	Reliant	Colt	Peugeot
Daimler	Rolls-Royce	Dacia	Polski-Fiat
Ford	Rover	D.A.F.	Porsche
Hillman	Sunbeam	Daihatsu	Proton
Humber	Talbot	Datsun	Renault
Jaguar	Triumph	Ferrari	Saab
Jensen	Vauxhall	Fiat	Seat
Leyland	Wolseley	F.S.O.	Simca
Lotus		Honda	Skoda
		Hyundai	Subaru
		Isuza	Suzuki
		Lada	Toyota
		Lancia	Volkswagen
		Mazda	Volvo
		Mercedes	Wartburg
		Mutsubishi	Yugo

Registration Letter and Year of Make

Registration letter at beginning of plate

G	89 – 90
F	88 – 89
E	87 – 88
D	86 – 87
C	85 – 86
B	84 – 85
A	83 – 84

Note
The new registration letter comes into operation on August 1st each year.

Registration letter at end of plate

Y	82 – 83
X	81 – 82
W	80 – 81
V	79 – 80
T	78 – 79
S	77 – 78
R	76 – 77
P	75 – 76
N	74 – 75
M	73 – 74
L	72 – 73
K	71 – 72
J	70 – 71

TRIANGLE TANGRAM

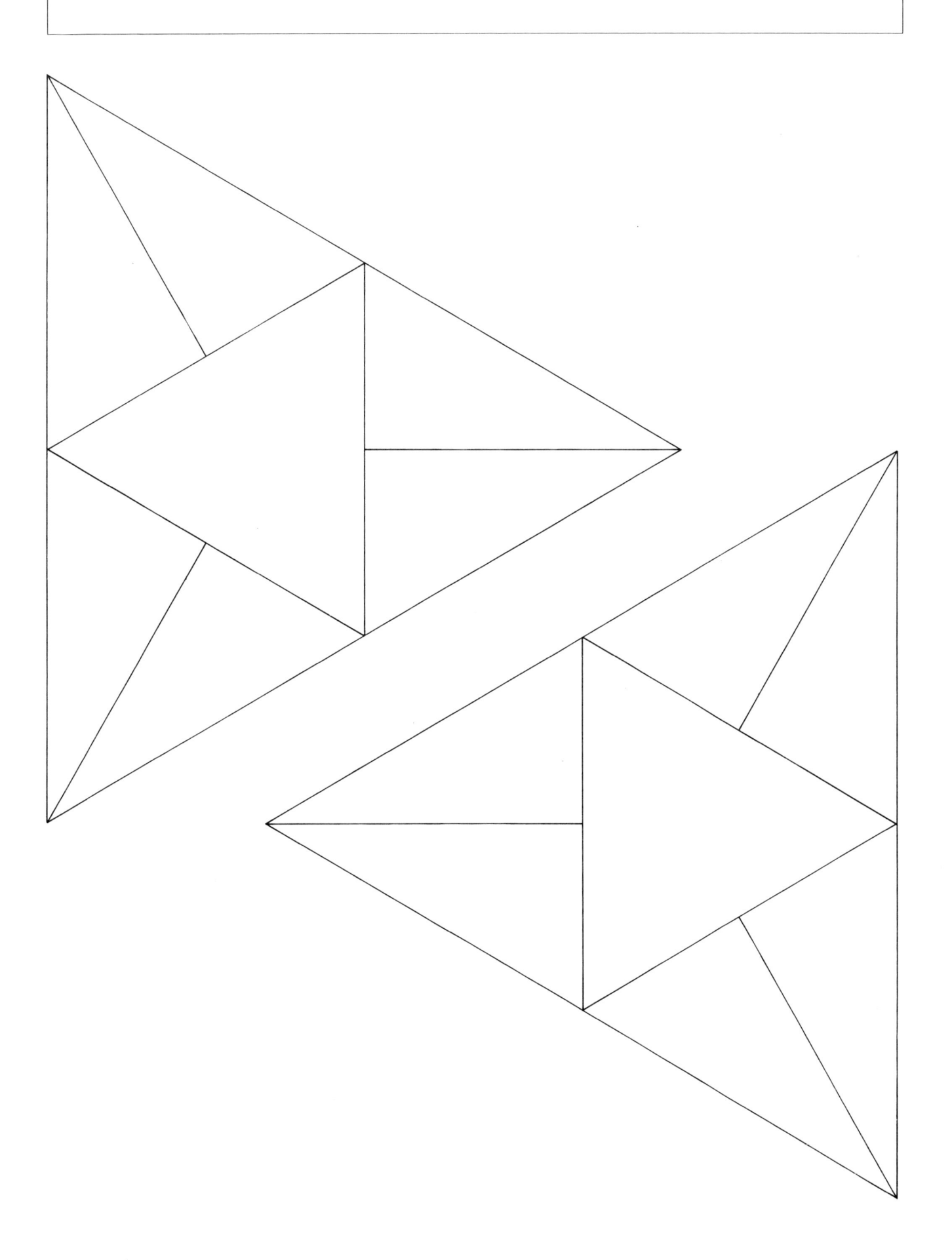

TRIANGLE TANGRAM

9b/2

TRIANGLE TANGRAM

THE WATER LILY

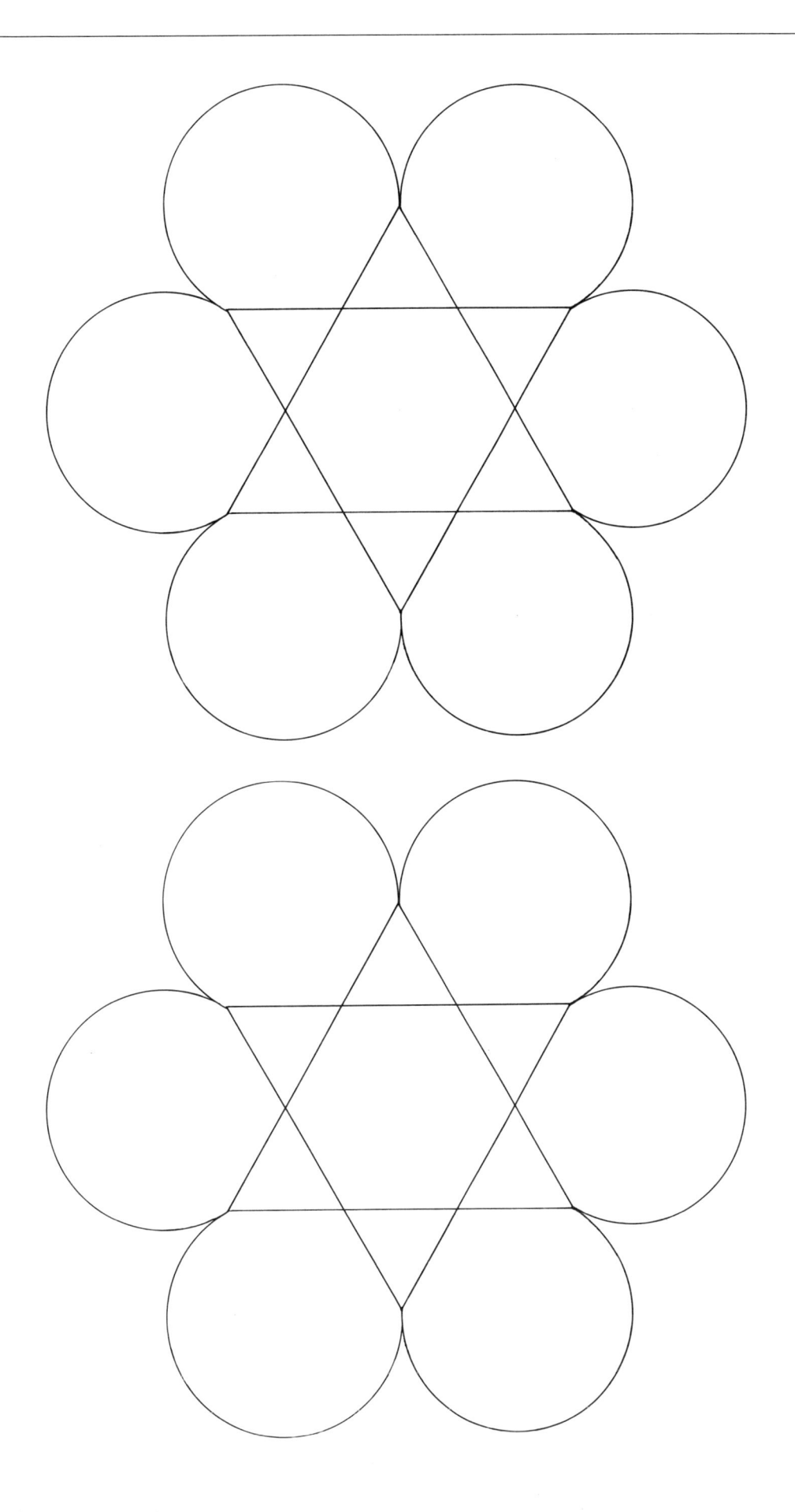

RADAR BATTLESHIPS

You have to sink your opponent's fleet

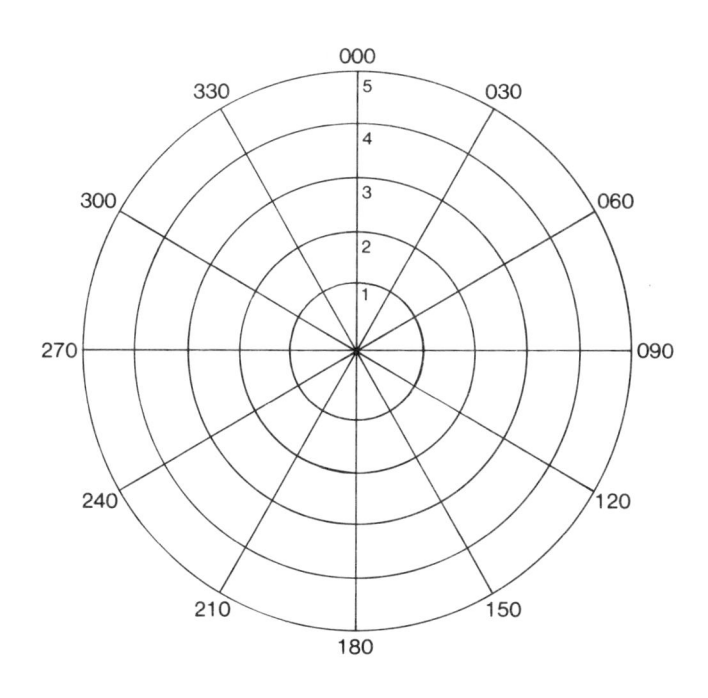

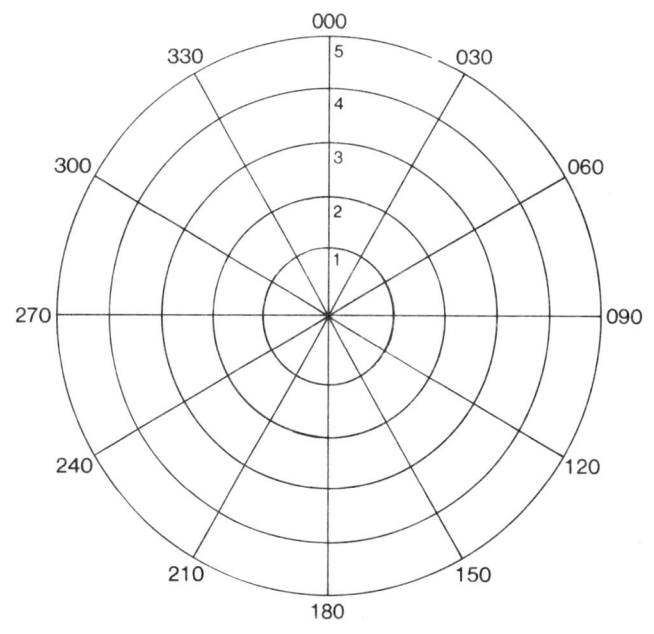

1. Mark your ships on one of the grids.

   You are allowed
   - 2 battleships — 3 points in a line for each
   - 2 destroyers — 2 points in a line for each
   - 2 submarines — a single point for each
   - 1 aircraft carrier — 4 points in a line for each

   (Each set of points must be on the same straight line or on a continuous arc)

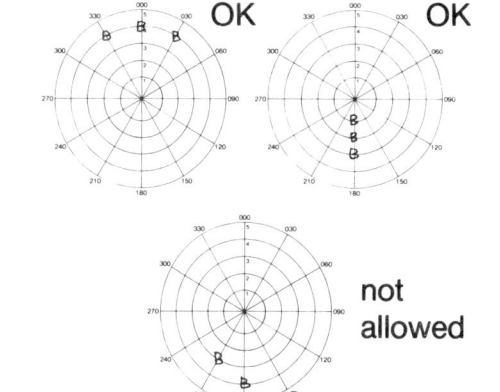

2. Decide who will go first.

3. Take it in turns to choose a point in order to find your opponent's ships.

   Direction 60 circle 4

4. Use your own grid to note your opponent's guesses.
   You have to say whether each guess is a "hit", "miss" or "hit and sunk".

5. Use the other grid to note your own guesses and hits.

6. The winner is the player who is first to find the other player's ships.

SCREEN LOGO

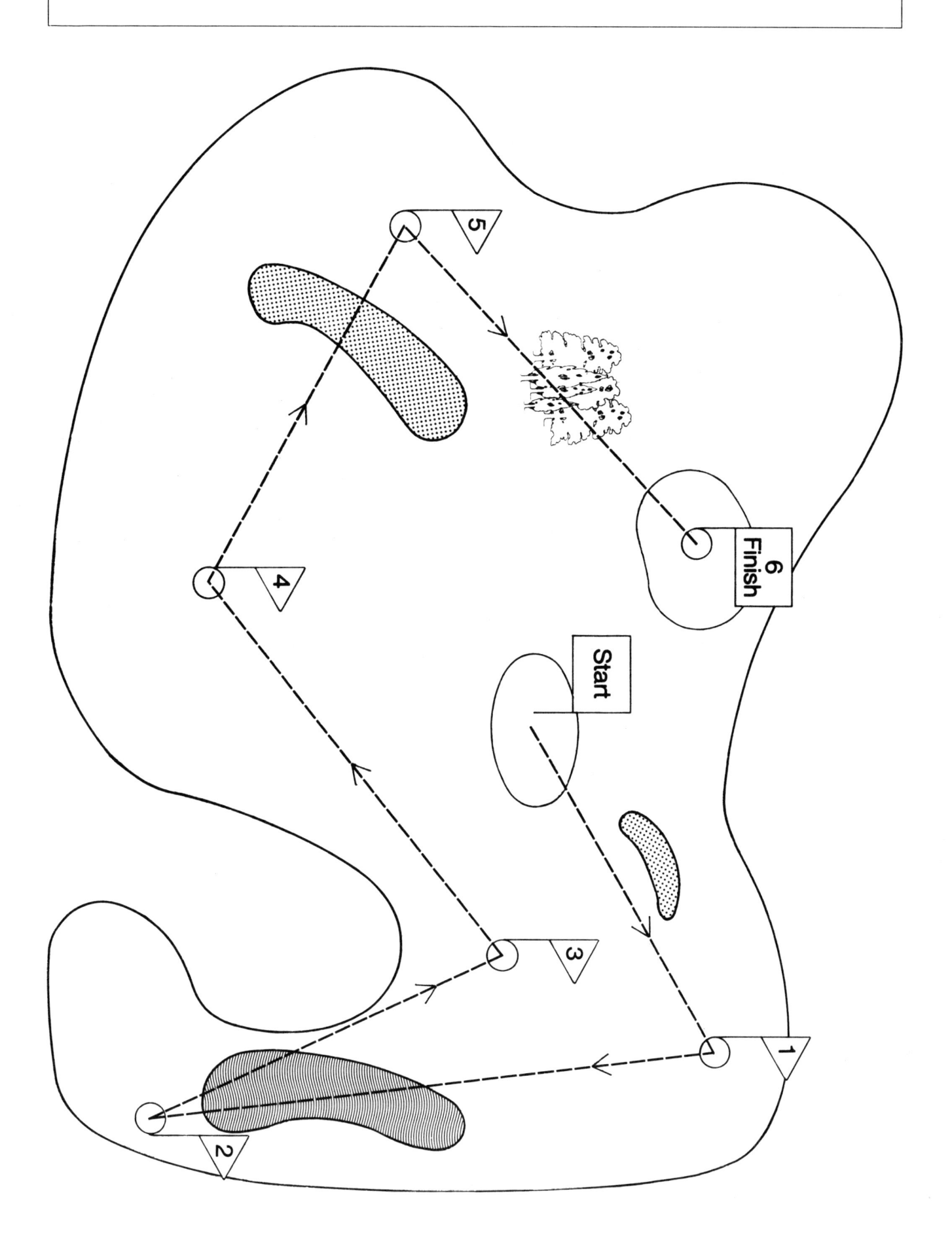

11c

12g

DATA COLLECTION SHEET

Name ....

SHOP

ITEM

TOTAL COST						

VOLCANOES

Volcanoes Name SLAMAT Country INDONESIA Area S.E. ASIA Height 3438 m Status ACTIVE	**Volcanoes** Name SUNDORO Country INDONESIA Area S.E. ASIA Height 3135 m Status DORMANT	**Volcanoes** Name MARAPI Country INDONESIA Area S.E. ASIA Height 2911 m Status DORMANT	**Volcanoes** Name VESUVIUS Country ITALY Area EUROPE Height 1219 m Status ACTIVE
Volcanoes Name STROMBOLI Country SICILY Area EUROPE Height 926 m Status ACTIVE	**Volcanoes** Name TACANA Country GUATEMALA Area CEN. AMERICA Height 4064 m Status ACTIVE	**Volcanoes** Name FUEGO Country GUATEMALA Area CEN. AMERICA Height 3835 m Status ACTIVE	**Volcanoes** Name SANTA MARIA Country GUATEMALA Area CEN. AMERICA Height 3768 m Status ACTIVE
Volcanoes Name ICH INSKAYA Country USSR Area ASIA Height 3607 m Status ACTIVE	**Volcanoes** Name KRONOTSKAYA Country USSR Area ASIA Height 3730 m Status DORMANT	**Volcanoes** Name ELBRUS Country USSR Area ASIA Height 5647 m Status EXTINCT	**Volcanoes** Name FUJIYAMA Country JAPAN Area ASIA Height 3778 m Status EXTINCT
Volcanoes Name KARISIMBI Country CONGO Area AFRICA Height 4578 m Status EXTINCT	**Volcanoes** Name MIKENO Country CONGO Area AFRICA Height 4505 m Status EXTINCT	**Volcanoes** Name KILIMANJARO Country TANZANIA Area AFRICA Height 5889 m Status DORMANT	**Volcanoes** Name APO Country PHILIPPINES Area S.E. ASIA Height 2954 m Status DORMANT

VOLCANOES

Volcanoes Name COTOPAXI Country ECUADOR Area S. AMERICA Height 5896 m Status ACTIVE	**Volcanoes** Name SANGAY Country ECUADOR Area S. AMERICA Height 5410 m Status ACTIVE	**Volcanoes** Name TUNG URAHUA Country ECUADOR Area S. AMERICA Height 5033 m Status ACTIVE	**Volcanoes** Name COTACACHI Country ECUADOR Area S. AMERICA Height 4937 m Status ACTIVE
Volcanoes Name PICHINCHA Country ECUADOR Area S. AMERICA Height 4789 m Status DORMANT	**Volcanoes** Name POPOCATAPETL Country MEXICO Area CEN. AMERICA Height 5452 m Status ACTIVE	**Volcanoes** Name COLIMA Country MEXICO Area CEN. AMERICA Height 3850 m Status ACTIVE	**Volcanoes** Name PARICUTIN Country MEXICO Area CEN. AMERICA Height 2774 m Status DORMANT
Volcanoes Name WRANGELL Country USA Area N. AMERICA Height 4269 m Status ACTIVE	**Volcanoes** Name LASSEN Country USA Area N. AMERICA Height 3190 m Status DORMANT	**Volcanoes** Name ADAMS Country USA Area N. AMERICA Height 4100 m Status EXTINCT	**Volcanoes** Name BAKER Country USA Area N. AMERICA Height 3580 m Status EXTINCT
Volcanoes Name CAMEROONS Country NIGERIA Area AFRICA Height 4069 m Status ACTIVE	**Volcanoes** Name MAUNA LOA Country HAWAII Area PACIFIC Height 4168 m Status ACTIVE	**Volcanoes** Name EREBUS Country ANTARCTICA Area ANTARCTICA Height 3794 m Status ACTIVE	**Volcanoes** Name SEMERU Country INDONESIA Area S.E. ASIA Height 3676 m Status ACTIVE

WHO KILLED DOC ROBBINS?

Details to be entered onto computer database

Forename	Surname	Smoker	Time of Arrival	Drinker
DAVID	ROBBINS	PIPE	20.15	YES
JANE	ROBBINS	NO	20.30	YES
ROBERT	ROBBINS	NO	19.30	YES
SARAH	SMITH	CIGARETTES	07.15	NO
ELLEN	JACOBS	CIGARETTES	07.15	NO
JASON	CONNELLY	CIGARS	08.00	YES
NASMA	AZIZ	NO	09.00	NO
IMRAN	AZIZ	NO	09.00	NO
PETER	HUGHES	CIGARS	21.15	YES
MARY	ROBBINS	CIGARETTES	21.15	YES
NEIL	SMILEY	PIPE	20.45	NO
MICHAEL	ROBBINS	CIGARETTES	20.45	YES

12j/2

WHO KILLED DOC ROBBINS?

You have arrived at Grantley Manor, the home of Doctor Robbins, a wealthy, kind old man. The doctor has been murdered! He had invited a number of relatives to stay. One of the guests has committed the murder. Your job is to find out who.

Some clues can be found by looking very carefully at the picture below.

There is a file containing relevant information about all the people present in the house. It is called DOC and you can ask it questions by using a micro-computer and database software.

One last point . . . The BODY was discovered at 9.15 p.m. by Mary Robbins.

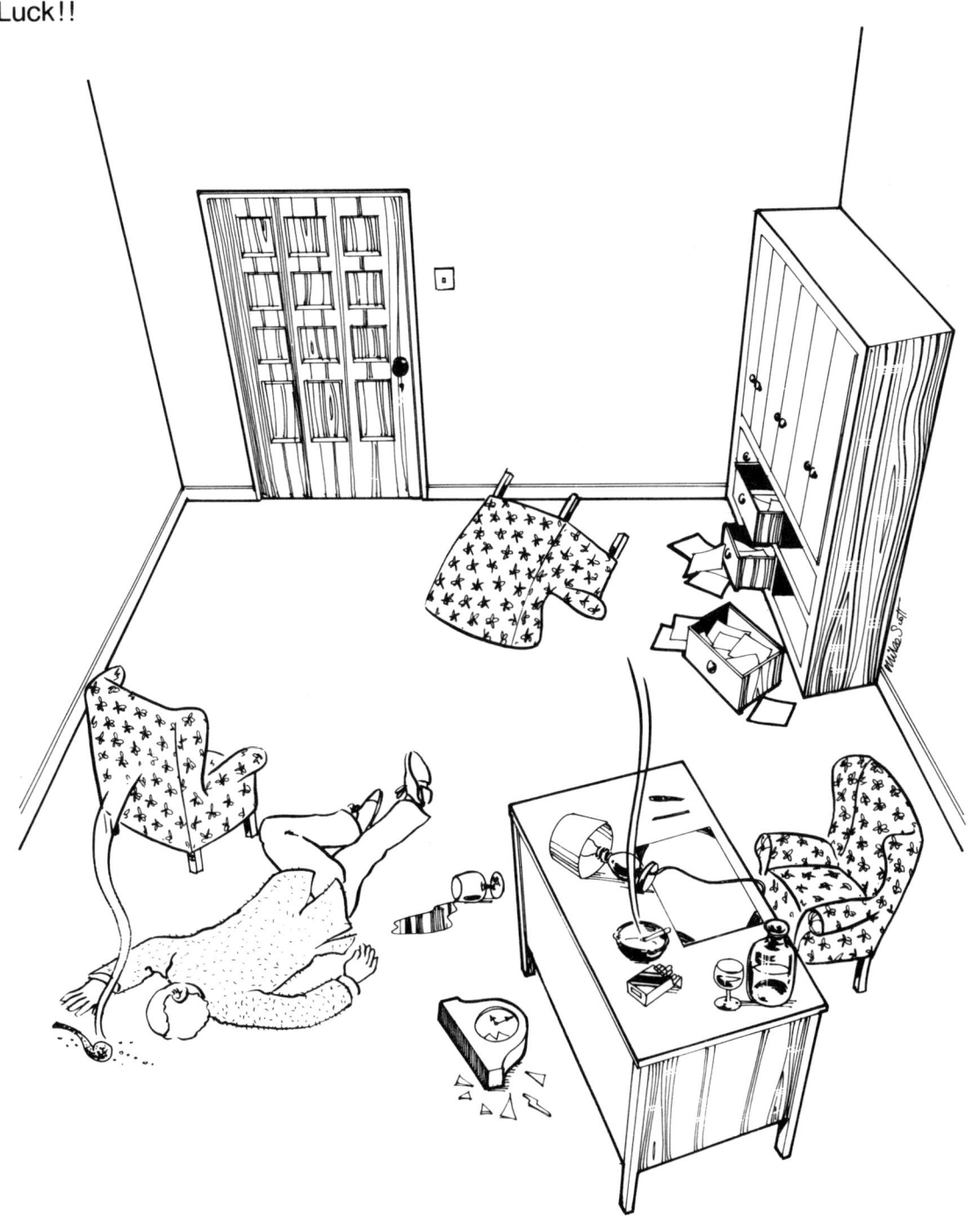

Good Luck!!

WHAT AM I? — a game for two players

WHALE	STARFISH	DOLPHIN	CRAB
OWL	LION	ELEPHANT	APE
CAT	DOG	RABBIT	MOUSE
BUDGIE	GOLDFISH	GRASS SNAKE	PARROT

ANIMAL SORT — an activity for pairs of pupils

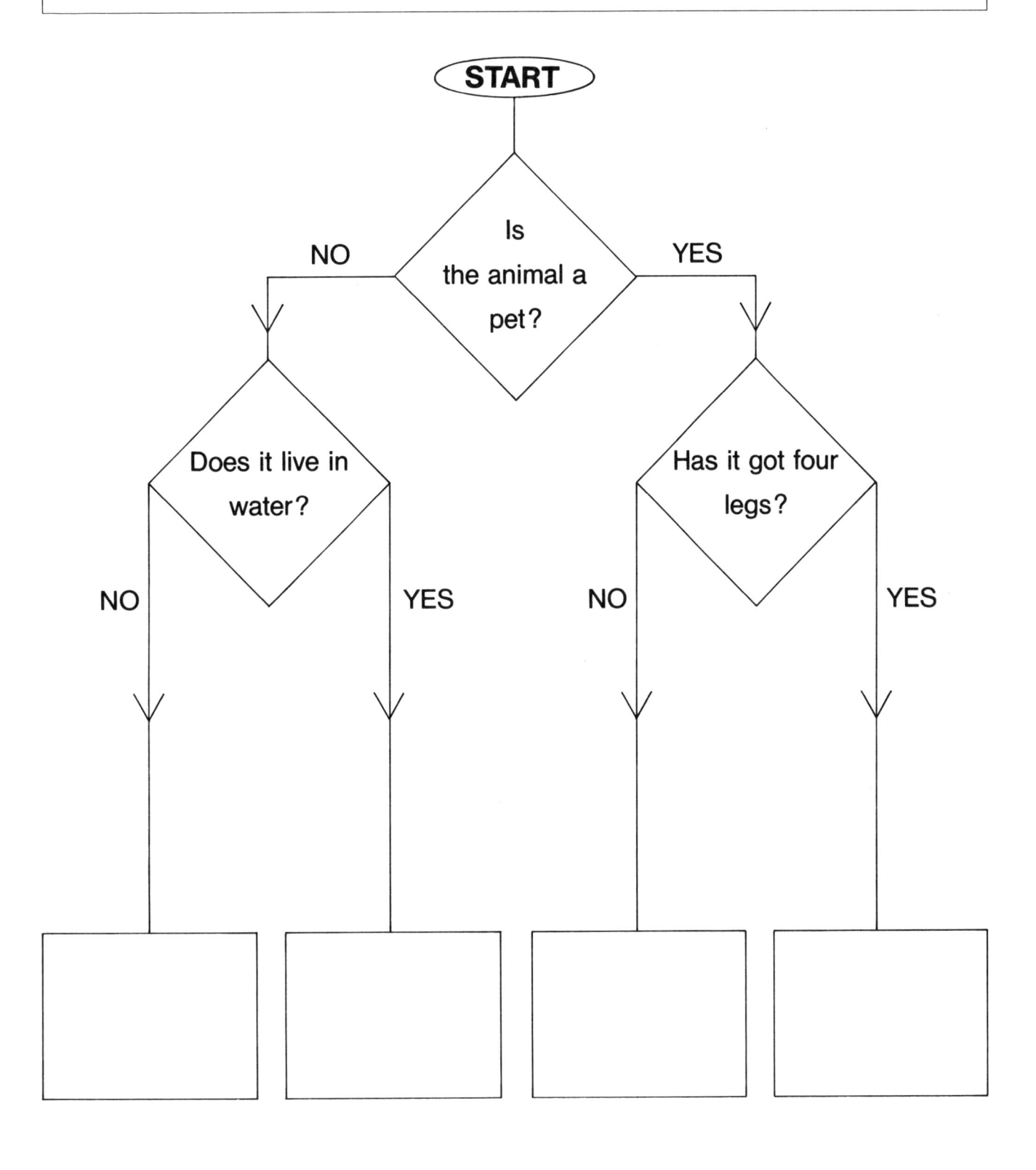

START

Is the animal a pet?
- NO → Does it live in water?
  - NO → ▭
  - YES → ▭
- YES → Has it got four legs?
  - NO → ▭
  - YES → ▭

13b

CAKE SHOP — an activity for two people

You will need: a die, graph paper

Record Sheet

Day	1	2	3	4	5	6
Cakes made						
Cakes sold						
Overall daily profit						
Cash at the end of the day						

RULES

1. You and your partner are setting up in business to sell cakes.
2. It costs £2 to make a cake.
3. Cakes sell at £3 each.
4. You have £10 to start your business.
5. Decide how many cakes you will make.
6. Enter the number of cakes made on the record sheet for day 1.
7. Roll the die to see how many cakes you sell. You cannot sell more than you have made!

   If you do not sell all of the cakes that you have made then the remainder must be thrown away at a loss to yourselves.

   Therefore at the end of the day it is possible to have lost money.

8. Keep a note of your daily sales on the record sheet.
9. Run your business for 6 days. If, at any stage, you have lost all of your money then you must stop.
10. Draw a line graph to show the amount of cash you have at the end of each day.

Remember you only have £10 to start with

*DAY 1 cakes made 3
cakes sold 3
you only have 3 cakes to sell*

*DAY 2 cakes made 5
cakes sold 3
Two cakes to throw away*

*cakes made 5 ... £10
cakes sold   3 ... £ 9
overall profit ...... £−1*

HOW MUCH PROFIT DID YOU MAKE?

DIFFERENCES — a game for two players

You will need: 2 dice and about 30 counters

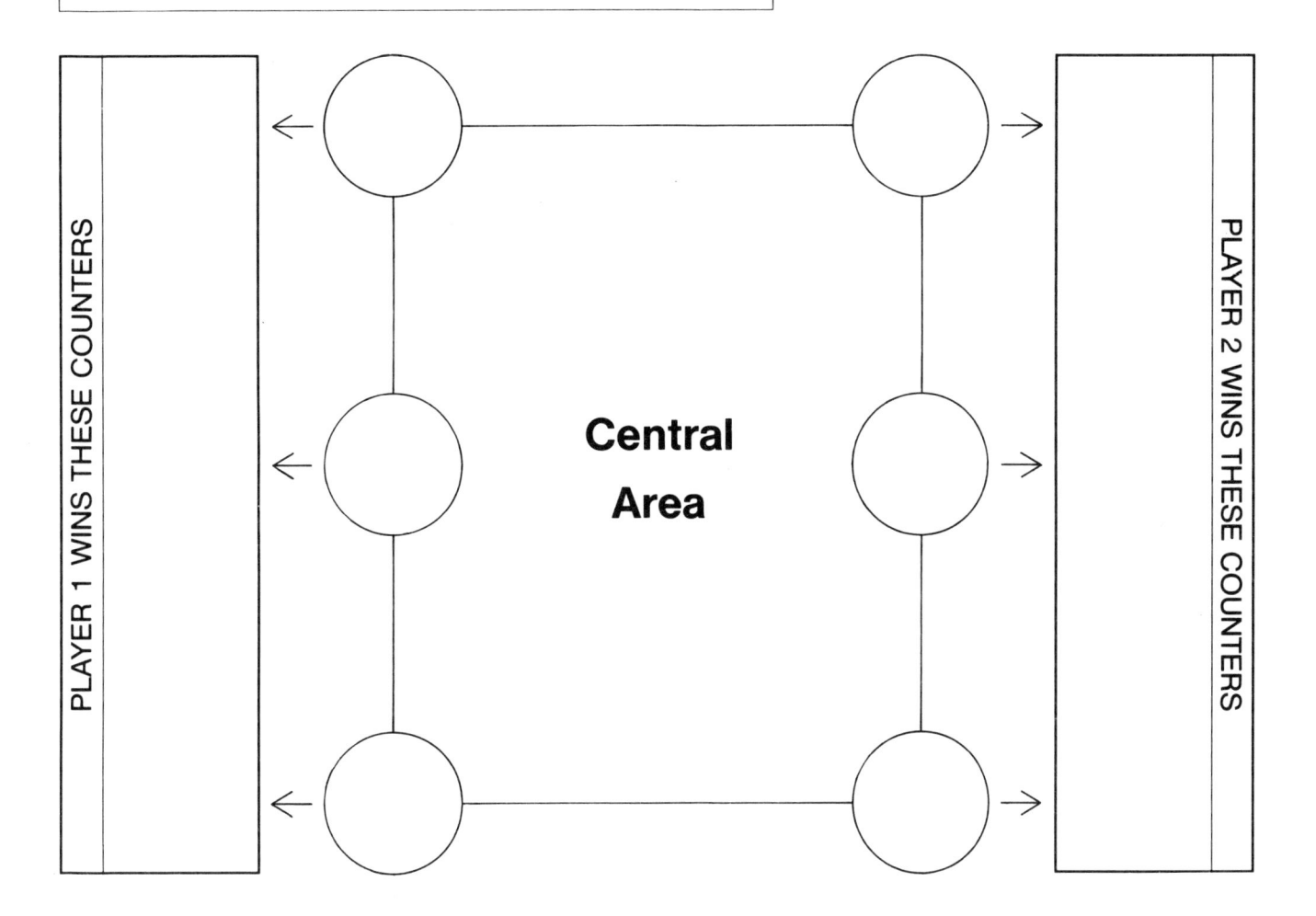

PLAYER 1 WINS THESE COUNTERS

PLAYER 2 WINS THESE COUNTERS

Central Area

RULES

1. Write the numbers 0 to 5 in the circles in the diagram, a different number in each circle.
2. Place all the counters in the central area.
3. Take turns to throw both dice. Calculate the difference between the numbers scored.
4. Move one counter along the arrow starting from that number.
5. The winner is the player who has most counters when all the counters have been moved out of the central area.

Play the game several times.

Do you think it is a fair game?

If you do not think it is a fair game then try to find an arrangement of the numbers 0 to 5 that does make it a fair game.

1cm SQUARED DOTS

1cm EQUILATERAL TRIANGLE DOTS

1cm EQUILATERAL TRIANGLE DOTS

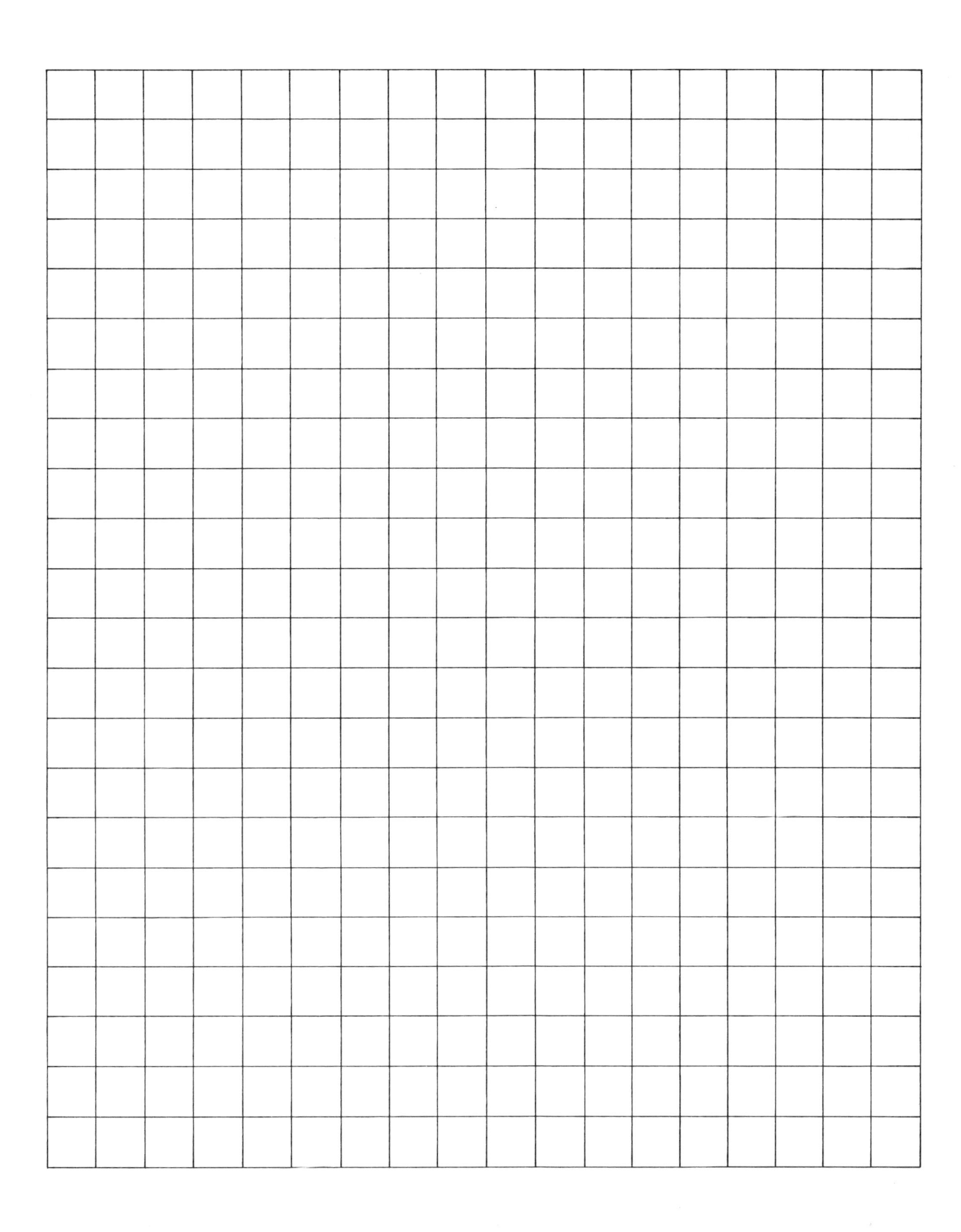

1cm SQUARE GRID

2cm SQUARE GRID

2cm HEXAGONAL GRID

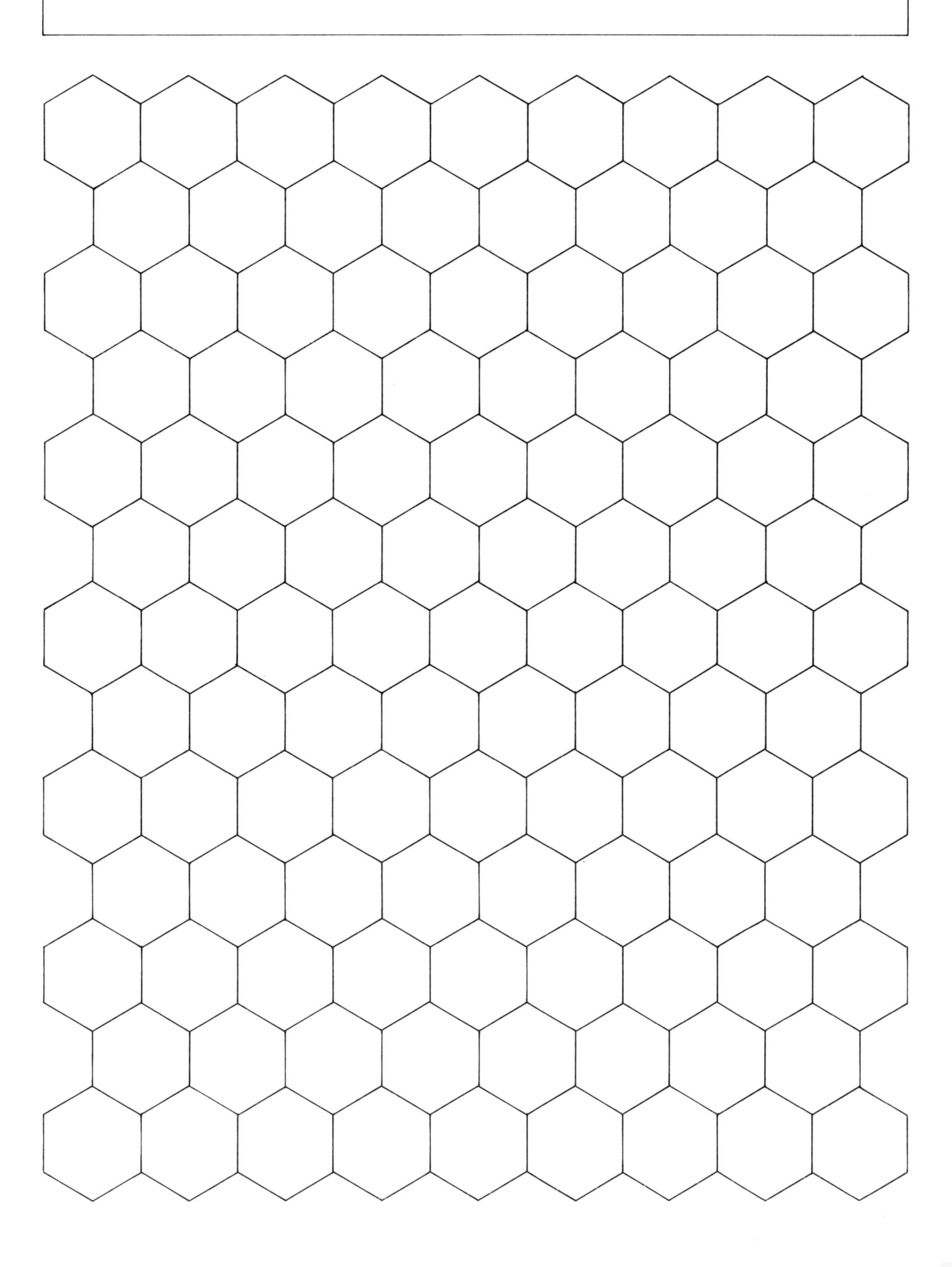